SURVIVOR:
My Life as a Haitian Refugee

Leferne Preptit

To, Mark and Family
7/14/2013

Copyright © 2013 Leferne Preptit

All rights reserved.

ISBN: 1484926137
ISBN-13: 978-1484926130

Published By: Prime Time Marketing
www.PrimeTime-Marketing.com

DEDICATION

To mother Marilia Sainnite Louisgeune, and my wife Melila Preptit. My mother was my rock and my everything. My wife always supports me in everything I do. Thanks for all your love and support!

ACKNOWLEDGMENTS

I would like to thank everyone who volunteered to take me to English classes. I want to thank all of my teachers who helped me over the years! I want to thank everyone at First United Methodist Church who helped us with our kids and helped us get on our feet in a new land! I want to thank Pastor William Fowler for welcoming us to First Church. I also want to thank Todd Saddler, Connie Creamer, Sandy West, Mr. and Mrs. Pastor Farmer for their kindness and support. Finally personal thanks to Mr. J.W. Hornsby for editing this book for me!

INTRODUCTION

My name is Leferne Preptit, and I was born on June 13, 1965 in the coastal town of Anse du Clerc, Haiti, in the Grand'Anse state. My mother, Marilia Sainnite Louisgeune, and my father, Emil V. Preptit, 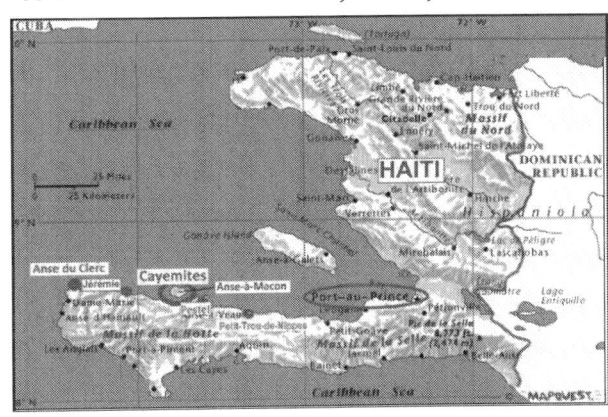 separated when I was about four years old. One year later, my mother and I moved to Anse-à-Macon, her hometown on the island of Grande Cayemites (just called "Cayemites"), just off the northern coast of Haiti's southwestern peninsula, and still part of the country.

Beautiful Anse-Blanche beach on Petite Cayemites

Haiti occupies the western third of the Caribbean island of Hispaniola, and the Dominican Republic makes up the eastern two thirds of island. One of the most beautiful beaches in Haiti is called Anse-Blanche, and is located on Petite Cayemite, a very small island just west of

Grande Cayemite. As you can see from this picture, this beach is like a paradise.

My mother and I arrived in Anse-à-Macon unannounced, and I will never forget that day as long as I live. It was raining very hard, and my mother and I were soaked when we finally got to her father's house. When the door opened, there stood my mother's sisters and her stepmother. They were shocked to see us, and after looking at each other and shaking their heads, they finally decided to let us into their house.

Right away we were told that my mother's father was in the hospital in Jérémie (capital of the Grand-Anse state, on the mainland of Haiti), and that there was no room for us to stay at their house. Someone contacted my mother's cousin named Ylora Louisgeune, and shortly she knocked on the front door and walked into the house.

My mother and I walked with Ylora in the rain to her house, where she kindly offered to let us stay in a room in her house for free. After a few months, my mother had earned enough money to start paying rent, and we lived there for about two years.

GROWING UP ON CAYEMITES

Since I was only five when we arrived, I basically grew up in Anse-à-Macon, which was the capital and largest village on Cayemites. When I was about 7 years old, we moved to a farming community called Nancarjour, where my mother and stepfather Megeune Odney 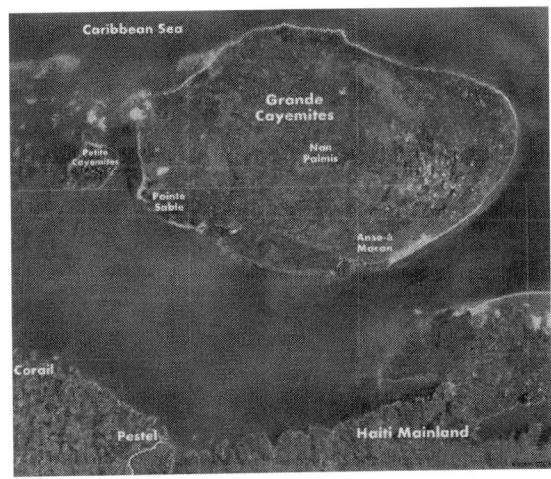 could grow and harvest their crops. Nancarjour was a 75 minute walk from Anse-à-Macon, and every day, five days a week, Monday through Friday, I had to walk from Nancarjour to school in Anse-à-Macon, and back every afternoon. That was two and a half hours of walking every day just to go to school!

Sometimes my mother did not have enough money to buy all my school supplies, so occasionally I had to borrow books from friends, or study with them and copy the lessons. As a child, I didn't understand what was going on, and I just thought this was normal. After all, I wasn't the only kid who didn't have all the books or notebooks needed for classes.

At that time, Anse-à-Macon only had one public school, and it was located in a rented building. The school did not have any computers or air conditioning. The parents had to pay a school fee, and also had to give a piece of wood to the school to built seats for the students. If a parent didn't have the money or the board to give to the school, their kid(s) had to stay home.

The school year started in October, but those who didn't have the money to pay the school fee had to wait until January to enter school. Some students stayed out for the entire year if their parent(s) did not have money. Some families with several kids could only afford to send some of them to school, which meant the others had to stay home. I remember going with my mother for over two years and I went to a place called Thomas-Ely to help a man harvest his coffee beans. It was the way she made enough money to pay for my tuition and to buy books, uniforms, shoes and school supplies. There were many kids in Haiti who were eager to learn, but simply didn't have the money - and thus the opportunity - to attend school.

I got very sick while I was in Thomas-Ely and almost died, but God saved my life! Mother never let me out of her sight, and she was always there for me. Sometimes people asked her to let me go stay with them, but she always refused. Even though we didn't have a lot of money, we had togetherness, and families helped each other and friends helped friends. The elderly watched over the children in the village, and the children were respectful of the adults.

My mother had four boys but lost one, and I was the youngest child. After my parents separated, my father had three boys and one girl, but tragically all of the others died. So even though I'm the only living child on my father's side, I didn't live with him. Growing up without a father to look after me made me subject to bullying, but my mother was always there to defend me. She was my rock, my bigger supporter, and my everything!

My mother did not know how to read or write, but she did everything she could to send me to school. She worked long, hard hours, and always taught me to be honest in everything I did, and to always hold my head high. She told me that my father used to say, *"Malere kon chen men mete yon kod sapat"*, which loosely translated from Creole means, *"poor like a dog, but always wear a sandal"*. Even though we were poor, my mother taught me never to steal, and that my word should be as good as gold!

I started working when I was nine years old, and made a promise to myself to stay out of trouble and always do what was right. I studied hard in school and was among the best students in my school. When I was in elementary school, I had to work to help my mother, because she got sick quite often. Sometimes I had to go fishing until late at night, and then go to school the next morning. Other days I went fishing after school and studied late into the night. In rural Haiti, after the sixth grade, parents have to send their kid(s) to high school in Port-au-Prince or Jérémie, which was very hard for most families.

I vividly remember the year 1976. I was 11 years old at the time, and the severe drought on Cayemites caused the farmers to lose most of their crops. People were starving, so I had to go to work to help support my household. Because I had to start working very early in my life, I did not have a normal childhood. My family did not have enough money to take any vacations. Instead, we constantly worried about one of us getting sick, not knowing if we'd be able to see a doctor, or have enough money to pay for school. Starting to work at such a young age was very hard on me, but I had to do it to survive.

As a working child, I was sometimes made fun of and rejected by my peers. But that did not stop me from staying positive and learning the value of hard work. Both of these character traits proved to be very important for me later in life.

CAYEMITES UNDER PESTEL'S THUMB

Though separated by water, the island of Cayemites was under the authority of the town of Pestel on the Haiti mainland peninsula. When I was a child, it seemed like the authorities in Pestel did anything they wanted on our island, and the people in Cayemites were not able to say, or do, anything about it.

For example, the authorities in Pestel came into Cayemites whenever they wanted - especially during the Christmas holidays - and killed the pigs, goats and chickens which belonged to the local families. Nobody could stop them, and if someone dared to say something, they would be beaten and jailed, and their families would have to pay a fine to get them released from jail. As a child, whenever I saw this injustice, it just ate me up inside, but I was powerless to stop it.

The farmers on Cayemites had to pay a yearly fee for their farmland which we called *"fem"* in Creole. This tax had to be paid in the taxation office located in Pestel. If farmers were not able to pay this fee, the authorities in Pestel came to Cayemites and arrested the farmers, then took them to jail back in Pestel. This meant that their families had to travel over to Pestel to pay the tax, plus the additional fee to get them released from jail. The Pestel authorities also seized everything they could find, including the farmer's crops, cows, goats, pigs or donkeys - they even stole their money!

One time, there was a missing child in the town of Anse-à-Macon on Cayemites, and the authorities from Pestel came over and rounded up everyone they could find - young children, women, men, even older people, and just beat everyone publicly.

Here's another example of the way the Pestel authorities discriminated against Cayemites citizens. A Cayemites man was arrested who at the time had a very painful staph infection in one of his feet. During the arrest process, one of the officers from Pestel purposefully stomped on his foot, which caused him to scream out loud, *"I have a staph infection, PLEASE do not step on my foot!"*

The soldier scoffed at his pain and replied, *"I do not care. It's not my problem."* Those injustices still haunt me today.

Later, I wanted to go to law school, because I thought that my best chance to help stop the injustice would be to become a lawyer. Unfortunately, I did not have the opportunity to become a lawyer, so instead I got involved in politics at a very young age.

POLITICS AND THE TONTON MACOUTES

My first experience with politics came in 1985 when my older brother Emmanuel Verdieu was arrested by a corporal named Richard who was stationed at the Haitian Army post in Anse-à-Macon. When I heard the news, I went to the Army post to get my brother released, where I learned that the officer had beaten my brother during the arrest. I was very angry about what happened to my brother, and decided to write a letter complaining about the officer. I took my letter to a radio station in Port-au-Prince called Radio Soleil ("Sun Radio") to tell the people and the government in Port-au-Prince about this injustice.

When the officer learned that I had written this letter against him, he became quite upset. He wanted to put me in jail, but the people in Anse-à-Macon were against it, and prevented him from taking revenge against me. Finally the Army removed this officer from his position. I was pleased to see that my letter had made a difference, and that the people of Cayemites had supported me. I had my first taste of politics, and loved it!

At that time, there was a paramilitary force called "Tonton Macoutes" which were created by Haiti's dictator President François "Papa Doc" Duvalier shortly after coming into power in 1959. These soldiers reported only to Papa Doc, and had the authority to use whatever violence needed to maintain order, and often tortured or killed anyone opposing the government.

The Tonton Macoutes continued to flourish under Papa Doc's son, Jean Claude Duvalier, who came to power in 1971 when his father died. Since he followed his father as President, the younger Duvalier soon became known as "Baby Doc".

The name "Tonton Macoutes" came from a common Creole myth in which an "uncle" (Tonton) kidnapped and punished unruly and disobedient children by throwing them into "sacks" (Macoutes), and carrying them off to be eaten for breakfast the next day. So children were obviously scared of these men, but they greatly feared by adults as well.

In January 1986, my brother Jean Rene Julot was playing dominoes with a Tonton Macoutes officer when they got into an argument. Before long, the soldier ordered two other

Tonton Macoutes to arrest my brother and take him to their local office known as the Macoutes General Headquarters. After they got there, they beat my brother and ordered him to pay a fee of 125 gourdes (Haitian currency).

After hearing about this, I went straight to the General Headquarters and told them what they were doing was wrong and illegal. They didn't care, and a fee still had to be paid in order to get my brother released. This made me very angry.

In reality, the Tonton Macoutes had a license to kill, and everyone was powerless to stop them. This time however, I decided to go to Jérémie to file a complaint. Jérémie is the capital of the Grand-Anse state, and the main office for all Tonton Macoutes in the state is located there.

So later that week, very early in the morning, my oldest brother Emmanuel Verdieu and I decided to take a boat over to the mainland to file a complaint against the Anse-à-Macon Tonton Macoutes at their Headquarters office in Jérémie. While we were waiting to board the boat in Pointe-Sable, the second-largest village on Cayemites, we were arrested by two Tonton Macoutes. They held us in the Macoutes office in

Pointe-Sable, where we spent the night in jail. They sent three Macoutes to Anse-à-Macon to tell the Tonton Macoutes there that my brother and I had been arrested, and were being held in jail in Pointe-Sable.

At the time, the Tonton Macoutes Chief in Pointe-Sable was Norveis Joseph, and when I told him what happened, he was surprisingly very kind to us. This was just the opposite however, of the treatment we received from the Macoutes soldiers. In addition to pushing us around harshly, two of the soldiers who had been watching us stole all of our money.

When the word arrived in Anse-à-Macon that my brother and I had been jailed in Pointe-Sable, the Tonton Macoutes Chief there, Nicolas Joseph, sent four Tonton Macoutes soldiers to pick us up. When I saw that one of these soldiers was Meridore Lafleur, I was very glad. I had known Meridore for many years, and in fact, he and I both had been given the same god-father at birth, which I suppose made us god-brothers. On that particular day, he was also a God-send, as he protected us and made sure that the other Tonton Macoutes soldiers did not beat us.

When we arrived at the Macoutes Headquarters in Anse-à-Macon, the office was filled with Tonton Macoutes soldiers. Chief Nicolas Joseph however, was away in another village called Aux Basses. Aux **Basses is located in the main land of Haiti in front of Cayemites**, so we had to wait for him to return. We watched nervously as the Macoutes soldiers were busily preparing rope, sticks and other materials to beat us. They accused us, especially me, of opposing the Duvalier regime, which at that time in Haiti was punishable by death.

When the chief returned, some of the Macoutes soldiers told him that we were "*kamoken-an*", a Creole term used by the Tonton Macoutes to describe someone who was opposing the Duvalier regime. Some of the more compassionate soldiers said, "*Just let them go home*," but others quickly shouted, "*No, let's beat them!*"

Other soldiers added to the mayhem by yelling, "*Let's kill these kamoken-an* **here**, *because that's what will happen to them in Jérémie anyway!*" Fear gripped our hearts as these shouts filled the air.

Some calmer Macoutes finally spoke up, and objected, saying, "*We cannot do this to Leferne, because he is a young man who has never gotten into trouble.*"

But the louder soldiers prevailed, and the next thing we heard was that they had engineered a plan to put us onto a boat going to Port-au-Prince. They were going to take us before "Baby Doc" Duvalier as someone opposing his regime. That would be a guaranteed death sentence.

When the word got out that the Tonton Macoutes were planning to take us to Port-au-Prince, where we would probably get killed by Duvalier, my mother lost her mind. Most of the people in Anse-à-Macon, including many of the community leaders, stood strong with us during this confrontation, which was very encouraging to both of us. When the Macoutes saw that the local people were revolting against them, they changed their minds.

Although the Tonton Macoutes backed off from their plans to ship us to Port-au-Prince, they still demanded money in order for us to be released. By then my mother had arrived at the Tonton Macoute office, but she didn't have enough money. The Tonton Macoutes told her that if the fee was not paid, they would go ahead and take us to Port-au-Prince in the middle of the night. Fortunately, a good friend of ours, and a strong supporter, lent the money to my mother, so she paid 150 Haitian gourdes for our release.

A TARGET FOR THE AUTHORITIES

From that point forward, I became an easy target for the Tonton Macoutes, and they watched every move I made. They called me a "*politician*", which at the time was considered a dirty word in Haiti because they thought you were conspiring to overthrow the Duvalier regime. My family was afraid for my safety, even my life, because they knew that the Tonton Macoutes could kidnap me in the middle of the night, and I might never be seen again.

The Tonton Macoutes were very good at terrorizing the local population. They took land from people, stole their money, and even raped their wives and daughters. The Tonton Macoutes were strong and in control, and their soldiers often got rich in the process, which helped bolster recruitment and mobilize support for Duvalier's regime.

Ten days after I was jailed by the Tonton Macoutes for speaking my mind against the corruption and injustice, Jean Claude "Baby Doc" Duvalier was forced to leave Haiti due to civil unrest. I did not however, seek revenge against those

Tonton Macoutes, but instead tried to get help to develop the island of Cayemites. For example, in the town of Anse-à-Macon on Cayemites, we didn't even have a local judge or a state civil officer, so I joined forces with other local people to bring these local offices to the island. We met with a lot of resistance from ex-Tonton Macoutes, and I even faced death threats.

Another time I got active politically was when I created a petition to send to the central government in Port-au-Prince, asking them to elevate Cayemites to the status of "commune". I worked hard across the entire island trying to get enough signatures, but it was not easy. When I asked one man to sign the petition, he told me, "*I have no interest in politics and don't want to get involved in Cayemites affairs.*"

Then he threatened me, "*If you say another word to me about the petition, I'm going to punch you in the face!*" Like many people, he was afraid of the changes we wanted to make in Cayemites.

Another example of the local resistance to change happened to my mother. She had become ill and was going to the mainland to see a doctor. After she had gotten onto the boat with other passengers, the boat owner told my mother to get off his boat. When my mother asked him why, he told her, *"Because your son is trying to force change on everyone in Cayemites. If he doesn't stop, he will get killed."*

My mother replied with a calm faith, *"God's will be done."*

She then motioned to everyone on the boat and said, *"You people should thank my son Leferne and the others who are trying to bring change to Cayemites. Everyone on our island used to get arrested and beaten up by the authorities from Pestel, but they cannot do that here any longer. You should be **grateful**, not angry.*

POLITICAL ACTIVISM AND RADIO

Right after "Baby Doc" Duvalier left the country in May 1987, I started an organization called ACJPC (Association of Youth for the Development of the Island of Cayemites). Its purpose was to help develop the island of Cayemites, fight against corruption and abuse, and stand against the violent suppression of democracy. There were ten founding members of ACJPC, and the first elected officers were:

- Leferne Preptit — President
- Blaise Saintyl — Vice President
- Amilitha Guillaume — Treasurer
- Vitha Joseph — Delegate
- Guerdes Dorimain — Counselor

At its peak, the organization had about 1,000 members, and we held open public meetings each Friday. We even started a musical group called "*L'union des Jeunes*", which meant "Union of the Youths".

As ACJPC founder and president, my responsibilities were to make requests for development aid, and to intervene through the legal system on behalf of local residents who were ACJPC members. I wrote many letters to organizations in Port-au-Prince seeking funding, including a foundation called FAES (Front for Assistance and Social Aid) and the

BID (Banque Interaméricaine de Développement) that was funded by the World Bank.

Another important way that I was able to bring about change was through radio programs. For example, when a female member of ACJPC was beaten by a caporal named Eddy who was station in the Army post in Anse-à-Macon, I sent a signed letter to Radio Haiti documenting and describing the incident. As a result, I was invited to speak on Radio Haiti about that beating, and I also talked about all of the injustice that the people in Cayemites suffered under the authorities in Pestel. Radio Haiti (later renamed Radio Haiti-Inter) was the first independent radio station in Haiti, and was popular because it was broadcast in the Creole language. French was the official language of the country, but most Haitians spoke Creole in their everyday life.

I had several other opportunities to speak on Radio Haiti-Inter to denounce the injustices committed in Cayemites, including an interview with the well-known journalist Lilianne Pierre-Paul. Like others on Radio Haiti-Inter, Pierre-Paul did all of her broadcasts in Creole, which people loved, but elite journalists thought her work was inferior because of that. Her goal however, was to give regular Haitians all the news - not just about Haiti, but the whole world. She once said, *"Because my programs were provided in their Creole language, the Haitian people became informed, even if they couldn't read or write."*

Like me, Lilianne Pierre-Paul was outspoken and critical of the Duvalier regimes, and even spent six years in exile away from Haiti, fearing for her life. I was lucky to have been interviewed by her, as she was very supportive. The interview was later aired by the co-owner of the radio station, Michele Montas Dominique, who along with her husband, was also a well-known opponent of the Duvalier governments. Having these two prominent women from the media promote my cause in Cayemites gave it a huge boost in publicity. I also spoke on many other radio stations like Radio Soleil, Radio Lumiere, Radio Metropole Haiti and Radio Nationale D'Haiti.

Despite the criticism from so-called elite journalists, Lilianne Pierre-Paul' was later rewarded for her work when in 1990 she received the **Courage in Journalism Award** from the International Women's Media Foundation.

ACJPC worked hard to provide better services and improve the standard of living on Cayemites. In Anse-à-

Macon, the largest town on Cayemites island, we built at least six latrines, and also installed the town's first-ever wharf. In addition, we put concrete flooring in the town's public school, and built the first community public place in Anse-à-Macon. I also took the initiative to start an open market in Anse-à-Macon much like a flea market. The organization was able to finance these projects with grants and donations from generous ACJPC members.

Another organization in which I participated was the FCCH (Formation of Christian Citizens of Haiti). This group was established before the 1987 elections to teach people to read and write, to teach them about the Haitian constitution and election laws, and to show them how to participate in elections.

I was a monitor in the FCCH program, and instructed a group of about 20 people three times each week leading up to the elections. The meetings were held in public, which meant that members of the military and the Tonton Macoutes had access to them, and knew the identities of the participants.

HAITI ELECTIONS OF 1987

I was president of voting station #1 in Anse-à-Macon for the election held on Sunday, March 29, 1987 for the popular ratification of the Haitian constitution. After the constitution was ratified by the people, I supervised the registration office of the city of Anse-à-Macon, as well as voting station #1 for the November 29, 1987 general elections. I was working under the authority of the Provisional Electoral Council (PEC), and my responsibilities included registering about 1,500 voters, counting votes, supervising four other members of the committee, and overseeing all voting activities in Anse-à-Macon.

Unfortunately, the 1987 Haitian general elections were disrupted by systematic violence, especially in the city of Port-au-Prince. About 10 am that day, Ernst Melville, president of the PEC, announced on Radio National and Radio Soleil that the elections were called off because of the violence. Armed soldiers forced the polls in Anse-à-Macon to close, and they and their Tonton Macoutes allies harassed me and other election workers with guns, although nobody was shot that day. In the aftermath of this violent election,

Army General Henri Namphy took control of the Haitian government.

After General Namphy came into power, the army set out to crush ACJPC, and some Tonton Macoutes saw this as a second chance to get me, so they paid a man to have me killed. This hired hit man, was an officer in the army named Israel Pierre, sent four soldiers to look for me, instructing them to tell me that he was going to "*drink whiskey out of my skull*".

My supporters in Anse-à-Macon however, were on the lookout, and when they heard about this, they told me to go into hiding. For my own safety, as well as for the other ACJPC members, I decided to dissolve the organization and lay low. We burned all the ACJPC records so the army wouldn't use them to track the members down, and I fled to a nearby town called Petit-Trou-de-Nippes. Later I moved to Port-au-Prince where I would not be recognized.

Once things settled down, I went to Pestel with another activist friend to meet with the officials to discuss Cayemites. One official in the new government under General Henry Namphy asked us why we wanted to have a justice of the peace and a state civil officer in Cayemites, and why we wanted Cayemites' status to change to that of "Commune"?

We told him that as an island, Cayemites should not be dependent on a remote city like Pestel, and the people in Cayemites deserved their own judge, mayor and civil officer - so at least we could have birth certificates for our kids made locally! The official got upset, told us that we were too young to get involved in politics, then stormed off.

SUCCESS ON CAYEMITES

But we didn't give up. After a lot of persistence and perseverance, in 1988, Cayemites officially became a Quarter Communal in the Haitian state of Grand'Anse. As a result, the central government installed a Justice of the Peace and a State Civil Officer in a new government office in Anse-à-Macon. **We had done it!**

I was one of the original staff hired in the new government offices, and was named as the "*Commis Greffier*" which means Assistant Clerk for the Justice of the Peace in Cayemites. My responsibilities included recording the proceedings of the court, writing mandates, and handling the court fees. As a touch of irony, in 1994, the very man who refused to sign my petition - and threatened to punch me - became the Head Judge in Cayemites, and stayed in that job until he died!

During my country's first-ever national vaccination campaign, I was in charge of the vaccination post in Anse-à-Macon. The vaccinations took place on Sunday, September 11, 1988, which became an infamous date in Haiti for another reason.

THE SAINT-JEAN BOSCO CHURCH MASSACRE

On that same day, September 11, 1988, the Tonton Macoutes, the army and other "attaches" attacked and burned down Saint-Jean Bosco Church in Port-au-Prince, where Father Jean-Bertrand Aristide was preaching.

At that time, Aristide - who would later become President of Haiti - was a liberation theology Roman Catholic priest, and the church was packed with over 1,000 people worshipping at Sunday mass. On that fateful day, the gunmen killed 17 people and injured over 80 in a three-hour siege. Tragically, it was later discovered that the demented killers even ripped open the belly of a pregnant woman.

One week after the Saint-Jean Bosco Church massacre, General Namphy was overthrown by Lt General Prosper Avril, one of his former allies. Avril was a member of Papa Doc Duvalier's Presidential Guard, the group responsible for protecting him, and served as President of Haiti from September 1988 until March 1990. Much like his former boss Papa Doc Duvalier, human rights organizations accused

Avril of committing serious crimes and many human rights violations.

Needless to say, during the years that General Namphy and Lt General Avril were in power, no pro-democracy activities seemed possible because of the military, Tonton Macoutes and "*attaché*" repression. The "*attachés*" were paramilitary gunmen who were usually descendants - sons, grandsons and nephews - of Tonton Macoutes soldiers. Some of these attaches were even actual family members of Papa Doc and Baby Doc Duvalier.

In July 1990, I was among the founders of an organization called FADIC (Haitian Foundation for the Development of the Island of Cayemites). The purpose of the organization was to find funding for, organize, and promote development on Cayemites. FADIC had an office in Port-au-Prince, and had completed projects building latrines and installing irrigation, and helped advance agriculture, forestry, fishing and other areas of economic development. Unfortunately, after the coup d'état in September 1991, FADIC was forced to suspend its activities.

THE FNCD AND ARISTIDE

The most significant affiliation for me and my family has been membership in the political party known called FNCD, the National Front for Reform and Democracy. FNCD was formed prior to the December 16, 1990 general elections from an alliance of two parties, KID and KONACOM, and they joined together to oppose the Macoutes and Duvalier regime. Catholic priest Jean-Bertrand Aristide was chosen to become the FNCD presidential candidate, and excited by the possibility of positive change, I joined the FNCD party. In the mandate document to the right, the FNCD logo has a rooster in the center of the sun with four principal rays each pointing to one of the initials of the party.

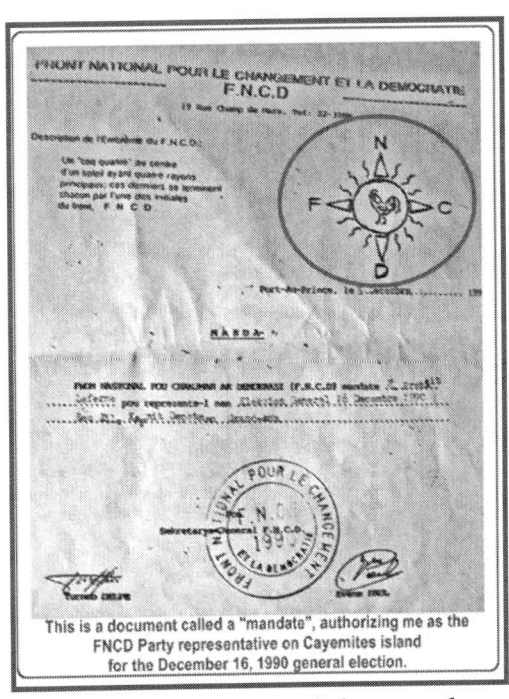

This is a document called a "mandate", authorizing me as the FNCD Party representative on Cayemites island for the December 16, 1990 general election.

While Father Aristide was the priest at Saint-Jean Bosco Church in Port-au-Prince, many Haitians heard him speak about the problems in Haiti, and how the country's wealth was being taken away. Many people had urged him to run for public office because the Duvalierists were so strong, and the constitution was not being respected. Haitians needed someone to rally behind, and at that time nearly everyone who wanted change supported Aristide.

When I heard about Aristide and FNCD on the radio, I traveled to Port-au-Prince on my own initiative to visit the FNCD headquarters and speak with the leadership. Shortly thereafter, my wife Melila and I were selected to serve the FNCD Party as "mandateurs", or official representatives. Below are the responsibilities my wife and I had as FNCD mandateurs:

- Recruit new party members
- Encourage them to vote for Aristide and other FNCD candidates
- Participate in setting up voting stations
- Observe and regulate all election activities in our area
- Uphold the electoral laws of Haiti
- Take legal action against election fraud according to 1978 constitution

Below is my actual mandate document from the FNCD Party - with translation to the side - which officially authorizes me to perform the duties shown above.

I, the undersigned, Mr. Mezile Justin, public surveyor living and dwelling at the town of Jérémie, identified by number 115-12-797-89***** for this present exercise, candidate for the senate of the Republic Haiti for the Department Grand-Anse, mandate Mr. Leferne Preptit, living at the town of Anse-à-Macon, to represent me in the December 16, 1990 election.

In this capacity as mandateur, he is authorized to pursue and account for whatsoever general election activities, to take part in the formation of the polling places, to make all propositions or objections deemed necessary, to undertake all actions proving to be useful to my candidature, in conformity to the prescriptions of the constitution and the electoral laws in effect.

At Jérémie, December 5th 1990

(Signed) Mr. Justin Mezile

During the campaign, I spoke in many different public places throughout the island of Cayemites and distributed campaign literature. I spoke about Aristide and other FNCD candidates, and about the need for real change in Haiti. I also fielded questions from the crowd, which included Army soldiers and Tonton Macoutes. There were also other attaches attending in civilian dress, which was pointed out to me by my associates. My job at the Justice Department, together with these political activities, clearly marked me as an opponent of the corrupt and arbitrary rule of the military and the Duvalier and Avril regimes.

In June of 1991, after Aristide had been elected, I gave a television interview to Haiti's National Television Network in my hometown in Cayemites. Herold Jean-François, who was the director of Haiti's National Television Network under Aristide, gave me his business card (right) and assured me that my interview would be shown on air. During the interview, I explained what I thought were the major problems on the island at that time. I spoke about the political problems, the importance of having Cayemites elevated to the status of Commune a few years earlier, and the need for education and access to potable water there.

I also interviewed with several radio correspondents in the city of Jérémie, including Lucner Laguerre at Radio National, Oges Saint Jean at Radio Lumiere and Franckel Valentin at Radio Sun Soleil. This local publicity helped raise the awareness about Cayemites' issues, and also made me more well-known in that area.

When Aristide took power, most Haitians wanted the country to get moving toward progress. In April of 1991, I showed my support for the Aristide administration by putting money together with other people in Cayemites, and going to Port-au-Prince to make a contribution of 509 gourdes (about $102 US Dollars) to the Aristides government (receipt at right).

HAITI'S PROUD BUT TROUBLED HISTORY

It has been my opinion that Haiti has not had good leadership since it won its independence from France in 1804. When Haiti became independent, it was the first free black republic in the western hemisphere. Since then however, the people of Haiti have suffered a lot, mostly due to greedy and power-hungry leaders. **Haiti** was once called the "Jewel of the Antilles" and was the richest colony in the world. Today, Haiti is the poorest country in the Western Hemisphere.

The Haitian people themselves however, have a heritage of bravery and honor. For example, during the American Revolution, 1,500 freed Haitian slaves came to Savannah, Georgia and Yorktown, Virginia and fought valiantly to help America get her independence from England. Among these brave soldiers were Christophe, Rigaud and Beauvais, who are well-known to Haitian school children as the "Haitian Heroes" of American independence. Haitians also fought to help Venezuela and Bolivia gain their independence.

This Haitian support of the American colonists however, would not be rewarded 141 years later. In July of 1915, American Marines landed in Haiti and soon thereafter the U.S. sent a draft agreement between Haiti and the United States to Mr. Philippe Sudre Dartiguenave, President of Haiti at that time. Feeling pressured to avoid military action, the Haiti Senate and Chamber of Deputies voted to accept the agreement. This meant that for the next 20 years, the United States occupied Haiti and had control over everything, including its natural resources and finances.

Shortly thereafter, in April of 1916, three decrees went into effect: one dissolved the Haitian Senate, the second turned the Chamber of Deputies into an Assembly Constituent, and the third one established a 21-member State Consultation. In June of 1918, a new constitution was approved by a Haitian plebiscite, which allowed foreigners to purchase Haitian real estate properties.

THE 1991 COUP D'ÉTAT

I was at home on the island of Cayemites when the coup d'état occurred on September 29th and 30th in 1991. I heard the reports on my radio, but wasn't sure if I could believe what was being reported from Port-au-Prince. There were no demonstrations or killings at that time in the city of Anse-à-Macon that I was aware of. Personally, I did not participate in demonstrations, mobs, or violent activities at any time.

Until it went off the air, Radio Kassik was reporting the killings as they occurred on the streets of Port-au-Prince. I could find no other stations broadcasting except for Radio National, which announced Aristide's exile to Venezuela. On the evening of September 29th, a Sunday, the director of Radio National urged the people to take to the streets in protest, but to watch out for the military. This director was arrested soon thereafter, which made the reality begin to sink in - the Aristide government had been overthrown.

While the coup was occurring in Port-au-Prince, the countryside was relatively calm. A provisional government took power in October and appointed ministers and general directors. Once this government got on its feet, it started to extend its power everywhere, and to gather information about Aristide's supporters. Most people believed that Aristide would re-assume power, and his supporters were anxiously waiting for his return. But quickly the military began to crack down throughout all of the provinces.

In November 1991, a close friend of mine told me, "*The Army is planning to arrest you, so if you don't go into hiding now, you could lose your life.*" I was expecting a military crackdown against Aristide supporters because I was familiar with Haiti's history of political violence. Specifically, I was aware of the exile and murder of many people who took a stand against "Baby Doc" Duvalier in the late 70's and early 80's.

I also knew about the 1964 massacre in the town of Jérémie in my home state of Grand'Anse. In Jérémie, "Papa Doc" Duvalier took revenge against the mulatto families who had voted against him seven years earlier, and some people in Jérémie lost their entire family. Since I knew about the political persecution in Haiti's history, I was anticipating a wave of retaliation against Aristide supporters.

EXILE IN THE WILDERNESS

As a result of the warning, I left my home with my wife and children on November 25, 1991, and fled to an uninhabited area in the north of Cayemites called Trou Angle. We hid in a cave in a semi-wilderness area, while friends visited us regularly and brought food. I also picked yams and maniocs from nearby fields which belonged to my oldest brother Emmanuel. Maniocs were small shrubs with edible roots which could be used in soups and stews, and they helped keep us alive during our exile.

While we were in hiding, a friend brought word that the army had come looking for me, and not finding me, they arrested my father, Emil Preptit, who had come to visit me at the time. My father was not involved in politics, and his arrest was a clear violation of Article 24 of Haiti's 1987 constitution, which prohibits the arrest of any person in the place of another.

After arresting him, they beat my father in prison, and he later died from his injuries. They also arrested my mother, Marilia Sainnite Louisgeune, and put her in prison as well. The people in the local community however, appealed to the army and the police on her behalf, and because she was a church member, they let her go.

I had a portable radio with me while we were hiding, and heard Aristide speak on the programs *Voice of America* and *Enrikiyo*. Aristide said he was in contact with the OAS (Organization of American States) and would soon return to Haiti. The OAS was established in 1948 to help member states in North, Central and South America and the Caribbean achieve peace and justice, and to defend their sovereignty.

After December came and went however, I began to lose any hope that Aristide might return. And as it became increasingly clear that the military was systematically rounding up Aristide supporters and their families, I began to think about risking an escape by boat, or any other means necessary. I now realized that I could never come out of hiding under the new regime. So having been assured that escape was possible, I decided to risk death at sea and escape to Cuba.

ESCAPING TO CUBA

Understanding our dangerous situation, a friend helped me and my family find space on a boat leaving Haiti on Monday January 21, 1992. That boat was later intercepted at sea by the U.S. Coast Guard, which took us all to a refugee camp at Guantanamo Bay, Cuba.

Since the coup in September of 1991, FNCD supporters have been persecuted all over Haiti. Party members have been beaten, arrested and killed by the military and the Tonton Macoutes. Some had gone into hiding, and many others had fled the country. I had been publicly associated with FNCD and every pro-democracy activity in Haiti, and had become known as an advocate for justice in my community.

This information was common knowledge and was also recorded in several documents (election records, TV and radio interviews) which could easily have fallen into the hands of the military. Because of this association and public recognition, I would have been killed if I stayed in Haiti.

Up until the coup, I had worked for the Justice Department earning $500 per month plus fees, which usually were more than my salary. I hired people to plant gardens for me, which provided my family with sweet potatoes, yams, yaka, squash, beans and bananas. I also owned a sewing machine and earned extra money by mending clothes for other people. In addition, when I caught more fish than my family needed, I would sell the surplus to others.

We were very grateful that the U.S. Coast Guard took us to a refugee camp in Guantanamo in Cuba. As part of the transition process at Guantanamo, an INS (Immigration and Naturalization Service) officer interviewed me, my wife Melila, and our four children. I explained my former government job in Haiti to the officer, and even showed him a paycheck stub and other documents I had with me. As the officer reviewed my papers, I told him about the situation that forced me to leave Haiti with my family.

"*So where are you going?*" asked the officer.

"*We're going to Cuba until Aristide returns to power. Then we will go back to Haiti,*" I replied immediately, confident that this would happen soon.

"*Good luck,*" said the officer, as he reached out to shake hands with me. "*And make sure to hold on to all of your documents - you will definitely need them again.*"

As I shook his hand, I looked up and saw tears of compassion rolling down his cheeks. The officer looked away, slightly embarrassed about being emotional during a business transaction. He wiped away the tears, then smiled as he helped us carry one of our children through the checkpoint. He then looked at our whole family, and bid us farewell with these heartfelt words, "*Good luck to all of you.*"

This touching moment gave Melila and I a much-needed boost in our trust of humanity, which had been reduced to rubble in Haiti.

GUANTANAMO BAY REFUGEE CAMP

Shortly after that, on January 31, 1992, we signed papers to enter the United States, but we still had to "wait in line" by spending nearly three months in the Guantanamo Bay refugee camp. The treatment at the camp was not very good; some soldiers were very nice, but others were less kind. Some of the guards talked in a condescending way to the refugees, and about Haiti, which was very hard for me.

Even though Haiti had suffered from many problems, we Haitians were very proud of our country, and proud of who we were. To go from being well-respected in my community for standing against injustice, to being disrespected by these guards was painful. The worst part was that as a refugee, I was powerless to stop it, and just had to stand there and take it. That hurt a lot.

Sometimes I felt like my struggle would never end. One question I kept asking myself then was, "Why *are they treating us like this*?" At that time, I had not experienced racial prejudice, and did not understand how it made people act. One thing however, that gave me courage at the time was knowing that Jesus himself was a refugee, and I knew in my heart that Jesus understood what I was going through.

In many ways, the refugee camp was like a jail. They put us in tents inside of a camp circled with barbed wire. And while the accommodations were better than our time in the wilderness, we couldn't go outside without having a soldier guarding us. The food was only about one notch above edible. They did not have a school for the children, and there was no playground for the kids to have fun and burn some energy. There were always two or three armed Military Police officers (MPs) standing around to watch every move you made. The only encouraging event was when Colin Powell came to the camp, and told us that he would do everything he could to help us get out.

FINALLY ... THE UNITED STATES

After enduring these conditions, on Wednesday, April 8, 1992, my family and I left Guantanamo Bay refugee camp on a U.S. military airplane headed to Florida. When we arrived in Miami, we were welcomed by people from the Church World Service (CWS) organization, and they took us to their local office. Founded in 1946, CWS is a cooperative ministry of 37 Christian denominations and communities across the United States whose mission is to "feed the hungry, clothe the naked, heal the sick, comfort the aged, and shelter the homeless."

While we were at the CWS office, I told a very nice female employee I had worked for the Haitian government. She reviewed our documents and listened to our story, then told me, *"Miami would not be a good place to stay and raise your kids. It would be better for our family to go to another part of the country."*

"But the only people I knew in the United States are two cousins near Miami, in Homestead, Florida," I replied.

She nodded her head and said, "*Okay, I understand. Then go to Homestead and spend some time with your cousins. If you like it there, you can stay. But if you don't like it, call me back, and I will try to find a place in another state for you and your family to live.*" She handed me her business card and said with a smile, "*Good luck!*"

So I called my cousin Sailande from the CWS office, and told him that we had arrived in Miami. He told me that he didn't have room in his house for us to stay, but said he'd contact our other cousin Louismable to see if he could help us. Before long I was speaking with Louismable, who graciously agreed to let us stay at his place. After getting driving directions, a man from CWS drove us to Louismable's house in Homestead. It was hard to believe that we were finally about to spend our first night ever in America!

We arrived in Homestead later that night with four kids and $12 in my pocket. In the morning, my cousin Louismable took us to a market and kindly bought us $52 of diapers, milk and food. As I looked at the passing scenes in the car, I distinctly remember seeing lots of people walking around Homestead with beer bottles in their hands, which bothered me. So after only two days in the Miami area, I decided that this was not a good place to raise our kids. I realized that the kind woman at CWS knew what she was talking about, so I called her up and asked for her recommendation for a better place to live.

"*I thought that you would want something else for your family,*" she said with a smile. "*I have two options for you to choose from: Bristol, Tennessee or Philadelphia, Pennsylvania.*"

I reacted quickly and said, "*I want to go to Philadelphia,*" thinking that a bigger city would have more people from my country.

She calmly replied, "But *Bristol would be a better place for you to raise your kids.*"

"*Are there any Haitians living in Bristol?*" I asked, with worry in my voice.

"*Yes!*" she answered quickly.

Knowing that she had been right about Miami, I trusted her instincts about immediately replied, "*Okay, we will go to Bristol, Tennessee! When can you send someone to take us to the airport?*"

OUR NEW HOME

We were soon on our way to our new home in Bristol!

On Friday, April 10, 1992, CWS sent a man in a minivan to take us to the Miami airport to fly up to Bristol. Unfortunately, we were late and missed our flight, so we spent Friday night at a motel near the airport. The next morning we boarded the first flight out of Miami to Bristol, TN.

We had to change planes in Charlotte, so when we walked into the terminal, we were met by an airline employee who spoke French. She had a large electric cart ready for us, and we were soon weaving in and out of people through a busy airport terminal. When we arrived at the new gate, she told us to find some seats right here, and that she would be back later to help us. She told us to NOT go anywhere else in the airport, but to stay right here.

After sitting for a *long time*, we became hungry, but did not know where to go to order food. We spoke very little English, so we were worried and confused as we sat there waiting. She finally came back several hours later, and told us that it was now time to board the airplane to fly to Bristol. We jumped to our feet and grabbed our bags, and as we boarded the airplane, I felt a surge of confidence in my ability to face the unknown.

Finally we landed at the Tri-Cities Regional Airport in Blountville, TN later that afternoon, and were welcomed by several people, including Todd Saddler (who spoke Creole), and Karen Bennett and Kathy Madigan, who both spoke French. They drove us to a home in Bristol, Virginia (Bristol is a split city, with one side in Tennessee and the other side in Virginia), where this kind woman had agreed to host my family until we could find permanent housing.

Karen Bennett was the local leader of a group called Bridge Refugee Services (BRS), a Knoxville-based nonprofit organization that was working with Church World Services to locate sponsors to help us. BRS got four local churches involved in this effort: First United Methodist Church in Bristol, TN, Lee Street Baptist Church in Bristol, VA, South Bristol United Methodist Church in Bristol, TN and Virginia Avenue United Methodist Church in Bristol, TN.

The first church we visited was South Bristol United Methodist, where Todd Saddler took us with him to worship on Sunday April 12, 1992. We also visited First United Methodist Church, where at the time Reverend William Fowler was the pastor. He welcomed us with open arms, and even asked us to become members of his church. As a result, my family and I began attending First United Methodist Church ("First Church"). At the time, none of the other three churches we visited had asked us to become members of their congregations, so Pastor Fowler was making a very bold move. But he did it for the love of God!

HELPING HANDS

After that, First Church took the lead in helping us, and our journey began moving forward rapidly. Before long, Karen Bennett set up a job interview for me at the Cozy Dozy clothing manufacturing plant in Bristol, TN, and another church member drove me to the interview. The interview went well, and I started working at Cozy Dozy as sewing machine operator the very next day!

The church set up volunteer groups to assist us with language skills, doctor appointments, transportation and grocery shopping, and also to help us with our children. The church was even helping us pay for food! We relied on others to drive us wherever we needed to go. We counted on Todd Saddler to help us translate because he spoke Creole and was willing to help.

We were in a new land and a new city, with no car and no language skills, and didn't know where to go for anything. What we DID have though, were some great new friends who helped us so much. We simply could not have made it without them!

For example, I didn't even know where to get a haircut, and my hair was starting to turn into an afro. One day, a man of color knocked on our door,

and spoke to us in French, saying that he wanted to help out by cutting my hair. He said that he'd seen on TV that First United Methodist Church was looking for people to help us, so he decided to volunteer. We quickly became good friends.

Like me, my wife also did not know where to get her hair done. One time my wife went to a hair salon where the woman put the wrong kind of curl relaxer on her hair, and it ended up worse than before she went in. This was frustrating for my wife, and she didn't know what to do.

CHALLENGES OF A NEW LAND

One of the big challenges at the beginning was simply shopping for food. We spoke very little English and had no vehicle or drivers license. Sandy West, another First Church member, kindly volunteered to drive my wife to the supermarket and help her buy food. Even though Sandy did not speak Creole or French, and my wife spoke very little English at the time, somehow they started communicating with each other through sign language. With lots of patience and laughter, Sandy and my wife managed to understand each other fairly well, and had lots of fun along the way!

Another church member named Connie Creamer also demonstrated her servant's heart by taking my wife to the grocery store. In addition, she gave us a great gift by helping us with the kids, which meant a lot when you had four young ones!

Since we didn't have health insurance, one of the employees at Church World Service in New York recommended that I go to VA Human Services to see if I could qualify for health insurance for me and/or my family through Medicaid.

Todd Sandler arranged for a church member to drive us to the Department of Human Services in Bristol, VA, but our application for health insurance was denied. Todd had previously told me that doctors can be very expensive here, so after we were denied, I panicked. I simply didn't know what I'd do if somebody in my family got sick. But I just decided to leave everything in God's hands.

Even though we had great support from our church friends, life was still very difficult for us. One day my wife called me at work and said she was sick. Right away I left work, and when I got home, she was already vomiting and just felt awful. Not having health insurance, I was scared and confused, but I didn't want to bother anybody. So I grabbed my French dictionary and went to the Rite Aid pharmacy in downtown Bristol, where I asked an employee to please help me. I pointed to the word vomiting in the dictionary, and tried to communicate that my wife was throwing up, and needed medication.

The employee quickly found the medicine I needed, so I paid for it and hurried home to my wife. After she took the medicine, she stopped throwing up, and started feeling better. Only later did we find out that the reason my wife was throwing up was that she was pregnant with our youngest son, Jeff Leferneson Preptit III!

Since our family was growing, we needed more room, so in July of 1992, the church and Todd Saddler helped us to move to a place of our own in Bristol, Tennessee. During that summer, Connie Creamer helped us enroll our children Manes, Nathalie and John at Haynesfield Elementary School in the Bristol, TN school system.

Two months later, Tommy Creamer - Connie's husband - got me a job at Bojangles' restaurant in Bristol, so I was now working two jobs and going to night school to better my English skills. I had two jobs, but still no health insurance.

Mrs. Creamer continued helping us with grocery shopping, schooling, baby sitting, doctors appointments, nearly everything. I was working, but did not have a car or a driver's license yet. Pastor William at South Bristol United Methodist Church asked one of his church members to help me learn how to drive, which he kindly agreed to do, even risking his own car with a totally inexperienced driver! Until I got my license and a car however, I still had to take the bus or walk to/from work.

IT WASN'T THIS COLD IN HAITI

I was trying very hard to adjust to our new surroundings, but the cold weather in Bristol almost killed me. Don't forget that I grew up in a country where the temperature almost never got below 70 degrees, even in the winter. Plus I was walking to/from work in the cold without a hat or a coat. To make matters worse, at Bojangles' I was working as a cook, and was constantly going into the walk-in cooler and freezer to get food, then back into the hot kitchen with griddles and fryers. After a couple of weeks of this routine, I became sick with a sinus infection.

After I got sick, one of the members of "First Church" took us to the Bristol, TN Department of Human Services to see if I could now qualify for health insurance and other assistance. Although I didn't speak enough English to understand everything that was said, the body language and facial expressions of the case worker made me feel uncomfortable. So I was not surprised when they denied my request for family aid and housing.

Since my wife was pregnant at the time, the state provided health insurance for her, and they also covered my daughter Nathalie, my son John and my daughter Marie. For some reason however, the state denied health insurance coverage for me and my son Manes. My sinus infection got worse every day, and I simply did not know what to do.

I asked Todd Saddler what I should do, and he advised me to go buy some nasal spray, but that changed my sinus infection from bad to worse. I was getting scared because my head was hot, and my body was cold. I didn't know where to go to see a doctor, and I didn't know how much it would cost. I was hoping for the best, but preparing for the worst.

One day later that week, I took the bus to the store to get some household items, and after getting off, I noticed a sign on a medical building that read "*Walk-in patients welcome, no appointment needed*". My sinus infection was still raging, so I decided to take a chance and walk in. I told the receptionist about my problem, and asked her how much it would cost without insurance, worried that it would be hundreds of dollars. When she said, *"$29,"* my spirits lifted. I could afford that!

After seeing the doctor, he prescribed *Flonase* and *Claritin D* for me. After taking the pills and used the spray, I started to feel better. And even though I was still sick, I continued going to work at both jobs. The volunteers from the church helped me with transportation, so I could attend English class two nights each week.

Over time, Connie Creamer became closer and closer to us. She treated us with respect and dignity, and we not only became very close friends, but we became part of each others' family. Sometime Mrs. Creamer would take our kids over to their house to play, and she even had her mother, Mrs. Helen Jones, come over to read to our kids.

In addition, another wonderful couple, Mr. and Mrs. Farmer, were extremely helpful to our family during this time. They provided much-needed assistance with the kids, doing whatever they could to help with our children. With me working two jobs, my wife was especially grateful for the help from the Farmers.

DELAYED WEDDING

I believe that there are three important days in everyone's life: the day you're born, your wedding day, and the day you die. Back in Haiti, we had been saving money to have a big wedding ceremony. I was planning on getting married the same day as two of my close friends - Blaise Saintyl, who was the State Civil Officer in Cayemites, and my cousin Annelyse Louissaint. We wanted our families and friends to get together and be a part of celebrating the second biggest day of our lives, but the coup d'état took that from us.

So after getting established in our new country, my wife and I decided that we wanted to get married here in America, but we didn't know where to buy a wedding dress. Fortunately, someone from the church kindly volunteered to sew a dress for my wife.

On October 18, 1992, six months after arriving in the U.S., my wife Melila and I got married at First United Methodist Church! Todd Saddler was my best man, and Mrs. Connie Creamer was the matron of honor. Although we could not have any of our Haitian family members present at our wedding, we DID have our new church family there!

It was a joyous day, but because we didn't have much money, we didn't have a dance at our wedding, and we didn't take a honeymoon. I believe one has to work hard to make a living. Being a refugee has taught me a lot. I know I have to work to provide for my family, and my wife and I don't want people to look down on our children as people looking for handouts. So I got married on a Sunday evening, and went back to work the next morning at 7:00 a.m. I strongly believe if you have children, you should work to take care for them. I admit however, that I would've liked to have taken a honeymoon after my wedding, but maybe we can take our honeymoon later!

On March 15, 1993, my wife started having labor pains, so I called "Miss Connie", and she and her husband Tommy Creamer came over and drove us to Bristol Regional Medical Center. Later that day she gave birth to our youngest son Jeff Leferneson Preptit III. Her insurance coverage from the state only allowed for one day in the hospital for having a baby, so we had to check out the next day. Miss Connie came back to the hospital the next morning and took us home because we still did not yet have a car. There was a bad snowstorm that day, and without Miss Connie's help, we might still be walking home through the snow with our baby!

Going home so soon after my wife gave birth scared me, and I was trying to put myself in her shoes. I thought, *"What if she has a complication, what am I going to do?"* This cut me very deeply inside, and we all were praying that God would not let anything bad happen. I continued to go to school to learn English, and was hoping one day to find a better job, so that on my own, I could provide health insurance for my family.

POLITICAL ASYLUM

During this time, Todd spent countless hours helping us preparing the papers for political asylum, including driving us to Memphis several times. He did hours of research about the history of hardship cases in Haiti, and checked with Amnesty International to get more information about the coup d'état.

Also, Connie Creamer continued to be a huge help with the kids, and also drove us to Memphis several times herself. She spent countless hours with our children - she was at their soccer games, graduations, and birthday parties. In many ways, Miss Connie became almost a mother to our children. In 1998, she even went with my wife to Haiti to visit our families.

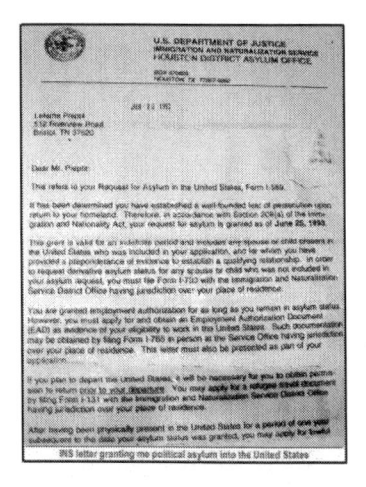

INS letter granting me political asylum into the United States

After countless hours from many people, on June 25, 1993, my family and I were granted political asylum (INS letter to right).

HEALTH BENEFITS ARRIVE

In 1994, almost a year after my youngest son was born, I went to a staffing agency and applied for a job. They sent me to Bristol Compressors on a temporary assignment, and after six weeks, I was hired as a full-time Bristol Compressors employee!

At the time, Bristol Compressors had very good benefits, including health insurance. This meant that my prayers of being able to provide health insurance for everyone in my family had now been answered!

Soon I was working 12-hour night shifts at Bristol Compressors, and some weeks even worked 84 hours. I was a man of character, and I always thought that it was my duty - not the government, or somebody else - to take care of my family.

As a hard worker, I wanted to get ahead, so every day I looked at the posted job openings within the company. Bristol Compressors had a policy that if an employee applied for a new position and did not get it, the hiring manager was required to tell you why. I applied for several posted positions, but did not get any of them. Sometimes they told me I was not qualified for the position, but most times I did not get an explanation. It always bothered me greatly, but I did not let it discourage me, and still continued doing my job the way I ought to.

There was one job situation however, that I just couldn't get out of my mind. I was working in the machine shop at Bristol Compressors and had applied for a job opening in the same department. I did not get the job, and was told that I was not qualified for the position. It turned out that the supervisor gave the job to one of his friends. A few days later, the shop Lead came up to me and asked me to help train the guy who had just gotten the new job. I couldn't help but ask myself, *"How could it be that I am not qualified to get this job, yet I am qualified to train the man they hired?"*

Later they started cutting hours at Bristol Compressors, so I got a part-time job at Pizza Hut as a delivery driver. I worked both jobs and went to night school, and eventually earned my GED and went on to college. Bristol Compressors had a policy that if an employee wanted to go to school, the company would work with their schedule to help make it happen. But for some reason, this policy did not seem to apply to me. I had asked Human Resources (HR) for this arrangement several times, and was denied again and again. Yet there were other employees working my same shift who got off early from work to take classes. It just didn't seem fair.

I had almost given up when one day, God sent a Good Samaritan named Charlotte Jumelle to work in the HR department. I went into the HR office one day, and told Charlotte that I wanted to go to school to better myself.

"I need my job because I have a wife and five kids to take care of and support," I explained. *"I cannot quit my job, and I had asked the company several times to work with my job schedule so I could go to college, but had been denied every time."* I added that I had even seen the company let other employees get off work early to go to school, but not me.

She firmly said, *"It is company policy to work with employees' schedules who want to go to school."* She showed me the right forms to fill out, and ordered the people who had been standing in my way to work with my schedule so I could take classes. I was so thankful to be able to continue my studies!

Sometime later, I went back to the HR office to thank Charlotte for her good deed, but was saddened to learn that she was no longer working at Bristol Compressors. I never saw her again, but let me say it here: *"Miss Charlotte, thank you!"*

UNSPOKEN BIAS

In many ways, my time at Bristol Compressors was a dream for me. While working there, I met some very good people, and it gave me the opportunity to provide for my family. On the other hand, it was also a nightmare at times. I encountered a few rude individuals who didn't seem to care for - or respect - anybody. I also had some great injustices done to me, and if I didn't have God in my life and His hand over me, I may not have made it through.

There was a culture of using scare tactics at that company to make people (me) look dumb, which made me sick to my stomach. I can't tell you how many times I was made the scapegoat and subjected to innuendos. I learned that one person cannot change a culture alone, so I had to go with the flow.

Here's one example. One time I was working night shift in the machine shop, and discovered that some bad parts had been run by someone who had worked the day shift earlier. The supervisor waited four hours after my shift started to call me into his office and tell about the bad parts.

I asked him, *"How long have I been running these bad parts?"*

He replied, *"About three hours."*

I challenged him by asking, *"If I've been running those bad parts for three hours, why did you wait so long to tell me about it?"*

He did not have an answer. And he also knew that he couldn't blame me for those bad parts without putting himself at risk as a supervisor for not catching the mistake for three hours.

For many days after that, I did not feel like going to work - not because I don't like to work, but because of how I was treated. But I had a wife and five children to support, and we needed the money and the health insurance. I knew that no matter what took place, I had to go to work.

Another example happened in the welding department. The welding work is done in two lines, A and B. I was working on line A when a gap occurred on my line. A "gap" happened when the assembly line did not have parts coming through, so therefore no work could be done. So while the other employees on Line A went outside and took a break, the Lead moved me over to line B to make me keep working. When the gap was eliminated, the other employees came back, and I was moved back to Line A again. The discrimination could not have been more obvious.

I went to the HR office to let them know about the way I had been treated on the welding department floor. Their reaction? They dismissed my complaint and acted like they didn't care - just business as usual.

Finally, after 12 years and 4 months at Bristol Compressors, I took a voluntary layoff and left the company, all because a few people had made my life a living hell.

COLLEGE GRAD AND FAMILY LIFE

I had worked two jobs - one full-time and one part-time - while I was going to college. In May of 2006, I graduated with an Associate of Applied Science degree in Computer and Information Sciences at Northeast State Technical Community College in Blountville, Tennessee. I was now a college graduate!

After leaving Bristol Compressors and Pizza Hut in 2006, I went to work at Wallace Mitsubishi in Kingsport as a car salesman, but didn't stay at that job very long. Shortly thereafter I got a good job at Citibank, which is where I still work.

My wife Melila and I have raised five wonderful children with good Christian values. We've taught them right from wrong, to stay out of trouble, and never to steal. When our children were younger, I had to work long hours so my wife could stay home to care for them. After the children got older, my wife worked two jobs one fulltime and one part-time to help us have enough money to meet our family's needs.

We've taught our children that nobody owes them anything, and that they need to work hard to earn a living. We believe that the most important thing in life is to believe in God, and have tried to instill that in our kids. All of our children were involved in church activities and did volunteer work in school and the surrounding community.

We also want our children to never forget who they are, and where they came from. We tell them if they stay in school and study hard, the sky's the limit. Finally, we don't want children to ever become materialistic and focus on their friend's nice car or money. We tell them, *"If you study hard and stay in school, then cars and money and other possessions will come later."*

We've taught them to always be grateful for what they have, and to not complain about what they don't have. All of our kids have played soccer, and the girls were also involved in dance. All of our children graduated from high school, and continued on to college. Two of our kids have already graduated from college, and one will graduate in May 2013. Three years ago we took out an equity line on our house to help one of our children pay for college tuition. Education is always a good investment.

My experiences in Haiti made me scared about the way a justice system can treat certain people, so I don't want any of my children to get into trouble with the law, or go to jail. To get this point across to our kids, I used to make them watch TV shows with young people locked up in jail. To compare that to a good example, I would also turn to C-SPAN and have them watch smart children wearing suits and ties, and speaking in front of Congress. After each show we would have a conversation, which helped teach them to be productive citizens, not statistics.

U.S. CITIZENSHIP AND HAITIAN HERITAGE

My family and I became naturalized United States citizens on February 17, 2000, and there were several First United Methodist church members there to celebrate with us. Even though I am now a U.S. citizen, I will never forget my background and where I came from. Haiti is my homeland, and is always on my mind.

There were/are many things wrong in Haiti, and the country's citizens have suffered a lot of injustices at the hands of their own people, and also by outside forces. Haiti is a not a poor country like the media or some people say. Haiti not only has a rich history, but also a wealth of natural resources. Plus one reality that the news media has not talked about is that much of Haiti's wealth has been taken away, either by other countries, or by its own corrupt government leaders who profited at the expense of ordinary Haitians. As a result, the infrastructure and government systems needed to run a country are weak or nonexistent.

When I said that Haiti is not a poor country, perhaps one may ask where I got this information. Just search the

Internet for the term "Haiti's Gold Rush", and you will discover that there's one gold mine in northeast Haiti worth $20 billion dollars!

Haiti also has many nice beaches which can attract tourists. About two years ago, an investor in Miami contacted me about developing Petite Cayemite island. I put him in contact with the Mayor of the Town of Pestel, and a resort is now being built on the island of Petite Cayemite where Anse-Blanche is located.

One of many beautiful beaches in Haiti!

THE SUFFERING OF HAITI'S PEOPLE

The people of Haiti are still suffering, so with the help of my church I had the opportunity to give back to my country. With Miss Connie's help and the support of First Church, we were able to sponsor two people on Cayemites to go to school to become health care workers. In Haiti, a health care worker is

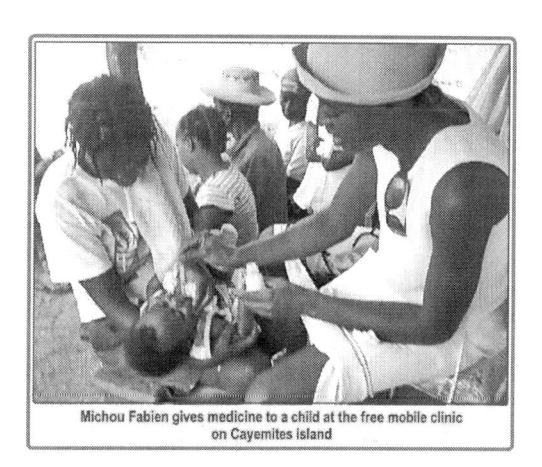

Michou Fabien gives medicine to a child at the free mobile clinic on Cayemites island

someone who cares for the sick and provides medications in the rural areas where people don't have access to a doctor. I know from first-hand experience how hard it is for families to send their children to school in Haiti. I lived there and know what those families are going through, which is why it's so gratifying for me to help kids continue their schooling.

We were able to bring medications, school supplies for the children, and sheet metal to repair public buildings in Anse-à-Macon. We also provided a free mobile clinic for the people living in the mountain-side town of Nampalmiste, and also for the towns of Pointe Sable and Anse du Nord. As I write this, we are sponsoring several young people there to go to school, because I know from first-hand experience how hard it is for families to send their kids to school.

We also went to Nan Palmiste, a town in the middle of Cayemites, and we provided a free mobile clinic for the poor and the forgotten. Miss. Michou Fabien volunteered to come with us, because as a nurse, she could do medical check-ups, take their blood pressure, and give them over-the-counter medicine.

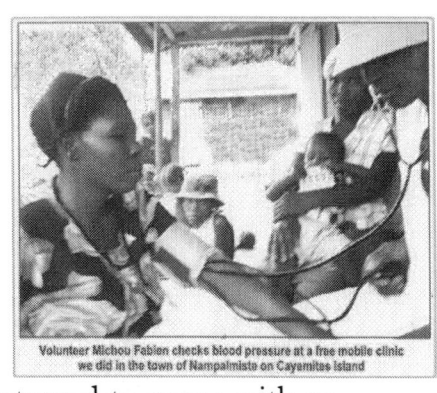

Volunteer Michou Fabien checks blood pressure at a free mobile clinic we did in the town of Nampalmiste on Cayemites Island

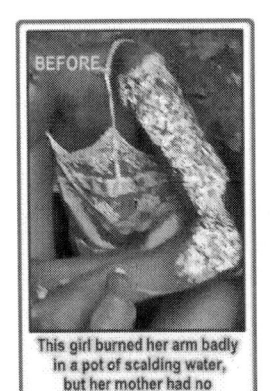

This girl burned her arm badly in a pot of scalding water, but her mother had no money to see a doctor

We met a young lady who had burned her arm badly in a pot of boiling water, but her mother did not have enough money to send her to a doctor. We were very glad that this mother brought her daughter to the free mobile clinic we were operating in Anse-à-Macon, where Miss Thomassine Pierre, a nurse-in-training, led the team helping her.

They cleaned her burned arm and applied medicine to it, and in just a short time, her burn looked much better. I also arranged for her mother to take her daughter to a doctor in Corail, a town on the mainland about three hours by boat from Cayemites. Several Cuban doctors practice medicine in Corail and help poor families.

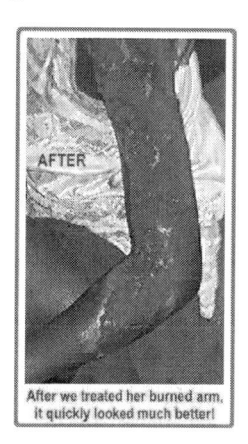

After we treated her burned arm, it quickly looked much better!

THE 2010 EARTHQUAKE

After the earthquake in January of 2010, the situation in Haiti changed from bad to worse. I saw countless people dying in the streets and many others buried alive under debris, unable to be rescued. That hit me like a ton of bricks, as I had family still living in Haiti, including my mother in Port-au-Prince.

I was not able to hear from anyone in Haiti after the earthquake since most phone lines had been severed. I spent many sleepless nights worrying, when after two or three days, a friend called and told me that my mother was still alive! Later that day I was finally able to speak with my mother on the phone. Though brief - only about 10 to 15 seconds - I was very relieved to hear her say, *"We're okay, I'm alive."*

My wife and I approached First Church about helping, and the pastor agreed that the church would send relief to Haiti. We went to the local television station WCYB in Bristol, Virginia, and the meteorologist Dave Dierks arranged an interview with the TV station for us We also were able to get an interview with Nate Morabito at TV station WJHL. On these interviews, we were able to describe the gruesome situation in Haiti. We signed up volunteers, collected donations, and had a cookout fundraiser. The funds collected by the church allowed us to fly to Haiti and set up an Emergency Shelter for children and other victims of the earthquake.

When I arrived in Haiti, I could not believe my eyes - the devastation was unreal. The workers and helpers worked tirelessly and were heroic, and I personally witnessed several rescues. I met men and women who lost their entire business. I saw people who were starving, and met many children who lost both parents. I hugged and cried with people who lost everything.

And sadly, on February 23, 2010, just 42 days after the earthquake hit Haiti, my mother passed away. She had given birth to me, but took her last breath in my arms.

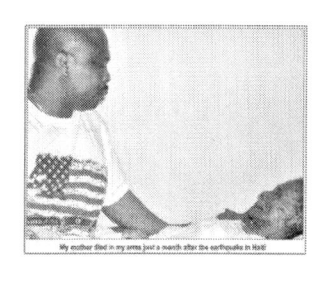

My mother died in my arms just a month after the earthquake in Haiti.

After my mother passed away, we set up a shelter in the house where she used to live. The shelter is now moving to a different location, but the program is still ongoing.

We met a lot of people who were wondering what the future would hold for them. I saw grown men and women crying like babies because their lives were ruined. Business professionals, who normally were able to take care of their families, were reduced to beggars.

We met a lot of mothers who did not know what to do with their children, who were living in torn tents - tents that leaked water, mosquitoes and germs, and as a result, many of them were sick. They had nowhere else to go, so they simply stayed there with their children and tried to survive. Sometimes these pictures bother me so much that I cannot sleep at night. Many times I have asked myself, *"What would I do if my children were there? And what would Jesus say to us if He was here in person?"*

To the left you see the refugee camp at Guantanamo, Cuba, which is where my family and I once stayed.

When I saw these children not being able to go to school, I could really identify with them. These people are refugees in their own homeland. ***We must help them!***

After the earthquake, Leferne Preptit speaks at the Guantanamo, Cuba refugee camp, where he once stayed with his family before coming to the U.S.

I am part of a group called ***Help for Haiti Children's Shelter***, and with the donations to that cause, we have provided food, education, supervision, clean clothes, and the opportunity to go to a private school with well-to-do Haitian children. At one point we were able to help nineteen children go to school in Port-au-Prince. We were able to meet with the director of the Red Cross in Haiti, and provide scholarships for nine additional children who are living in Tent cities in Port-au-Prince.

All of this happened because of the support of First United Methodist Church and the hard work of many volunteers.

Pastor Joe-d DowlingSoka, currently the pastor at First United Methodist Church, has worked tirelessly to keep the program going. In March of 2012, "Pastor Joe-d" went to Haiti with me to meet the kids we were helping, and to see how the project was coming along. The pastor was very pleased with what he saw, especially that all of the kids were now enrolled in a private Christian school.

I had to use my God-given gifts and talents to accomplish everything that was done. And I used my abilities to help less fortunate kids because I knew what it was like to be in their shoes, and do without.

FLASHBACK TO HUNGER

When I saw children in the streets after the earthquake who had nothing to eat, it reminded me of myself. It flashed me back to August 1982, when I was away from my mother, training in Port-au-Prince to become a tailor. When I first got there, I went three days without eating anything because I had no money. On the third day, I boiled salt, hot peppers and water, and drank it.

Later that day, I went to a small boutique where a friend named Alpha worked, and I asked him for some water. When he gave me the glass of water, I drank it quickly, and felt a little better. I was still extremely hungry, and knew that there were lots of shops nearby with food. But I had no money.

Just then I remembered what my mother had told me many times, years earlier: *"Do not steal, and do not get involved in anything you will regret in the future"*.

So I walked out of the boutique, still famished but with a fresh resolve to follow my mother's advice, and not steal any food. When I looked up, I saw a young woman named Ylia

Charles, who was also from Cayemites. When she saw me, she asked, *"Leferne, what's wrong?"*

"I'm okay," I replied, lying to her.

She quickly responded, *"Don't tell me that! You look starved! How long has it been since you last ate?"*

"It's been three days since I've eaten anything," I answered quietly, looking away.

She started crying, and reached into her purse and gave me 5 Haitian gourdes, which I used to buy some food.

I can honestly say that Ylia Charles saved my life that day. So when I see people suffering and starving, especially children, it is very personal to me. I know what it's like to be truly hungry.

CONCLUSION: YOU CAN HELP

A lot of Haitian children who are living in tent cities are not able to go to school. Sometimes another family will pay the school registration fee, but they cannot pay the school's monthly fee.

Leferne Preptit inside the tent of a mother with six children, struggling just to survive

Thus the children are sitting in the camp wondering what the future will hold for them, hoping for a better day. I met one woman who was living in one tent with six kids, and she told me that they recently went for four days without cooking or eating any food. I just wanted to cry when I heard that.

Leferne Preptit holds little Aglancia's hand

Despite the problems and suffering, the children of Haiti are still laughing and hoping for a better tomorrow. For example, please meet little Aglancia, who we met when she was two months old. She is still living in a tent city in Port-au-Prince with her mother and grandmother. Their tent was all torn apart and leaked so badly that they slept under a smaller tent inside of the big tent just to avoid getting soaked.

During the day, it was so hot inside their tent that it felt like an oven. In fact, in the picture, you can see that Aglancia's grandmother was sweating noticeably from the heat. My family is still supporting this family, but we have not been able to move them out of the tent city yet. Every day I struggle when I think about their living conditions, especially the children.

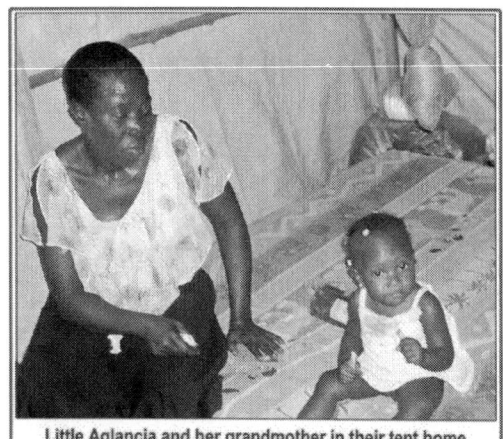

Little Aglancia and her grandmother in their tent home

If anyone wants to help us, please contact us, and we will be more than happy to give you information on how to help the struggling families in Haiti. I don't know about you, but these images keep me awake at night, and I try to work as many hours as I can to help.

I would like to thank my wife Melila, who has always been there for me, and supports me in everything I do.

I also want to thank all of my children for listening, staying out of trouble, and finishing school. ***I am proud of you all!***

I'd also like to thank all of my teachers and tutors who helped me over the years!

I want to thank all of the volunteers who have supported us and spent countless hours helping us. God bless you all!

Most of the children in this picture to the right lost both parents, and are living in tent cities with other relatives.

Leferne Preptit with Haitian earthquake orphans

When you buy this book, you will help us go to Haiti and move some of them out of tent cities into permanent housing.

When you buy this book, you will help us support a single mother who is still living in the tent cities, waiting and hoping for a better day.

When you buy this book, you will help us give Haitian men and women a helping hand to start a small business to support their families.

When you buy this book, you will feed a family of five who haven't eaten in two days.

When you buy this book, you will feed your own soul with compassion and rich love.

When you buy this book, you will restore hope to a Haitian child who has none.

Please visit us at www.fedha.org, or email us at verdieu34@yahoo.com.

You can call us at 423-383-1796

Thank you, and God bless you!

Leferne Preptit

ABOUT THE AUTHOR

Leferne Preptit is married to Melila Preptit has five kids and holds an Associate of Applied Science in Computer and Information Sciences. He also speaks Creole, English, French and some Spanish.

Made in the USA
Charleston, SC
07 June 2013